HOW TO I̶ THE

PIANO

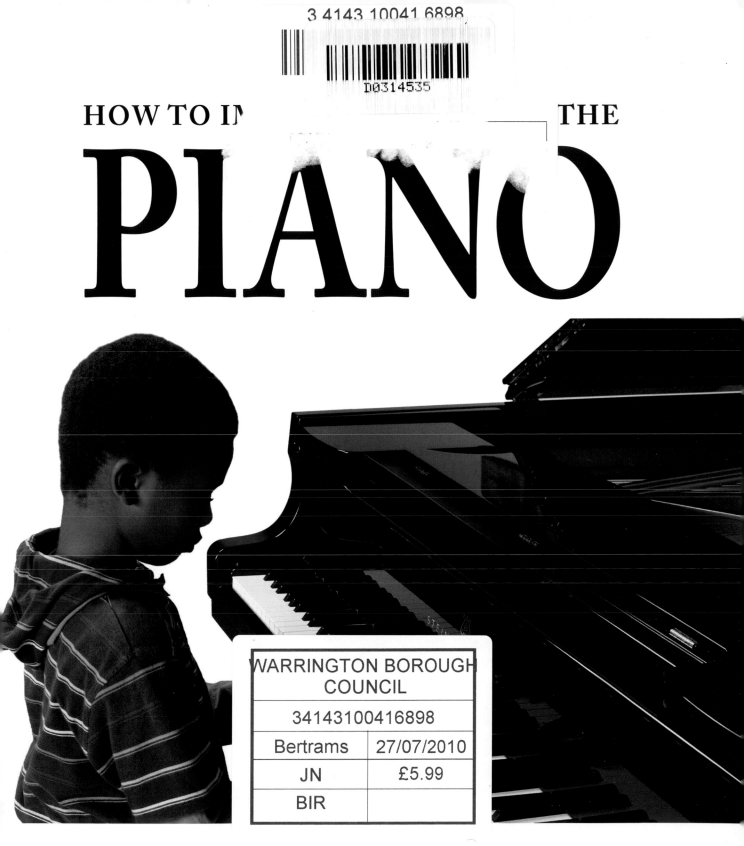

Elisa Harrod

Tick Tock Books

CONTENTS

STEINWAY & SONS

INTRODUCTION

Welcome to the amazing world of music-making. Music is something that is played, listened to and enjoyed all over the planet, whether it's dance music, traditional music, classical music or loud, crashing rock music! Being able to play and create music is a special skill that will bring you and others lots of pleasure. You're ready and willing, so let's take steps to improve your playing!

BUILDING SKILLS

This book will help you to build up your piano skills, running through the basics to more advanced techniques. On the journey through the book you will find new techniques and skills, and exercises to help you develop and progress.

HOW TO USE THIS BOOK

Nothing could be simpler! Use the contents page opposite to make this book work for you. You can work through the book page-by-page or leap forward to work on a particular skill or play a piece. Step-by-step guides help you get to grips with techniques and the custom-written piano pieces help you master them.

TOP TIP BOXES

Look out for these helpful boxes, which give you extra information on technique.

TECHNICAL TERMS BOXES

All technical terms and musical signs and symbols are explained in these boxes.

THE PIANO

Before you start playing, it is important to know something about your instrument and how it is set up. There are lots of parts to a piano and, although you may never need to use them, it is still really useful to know their names and what they are for.

EARLY KEYBOARD INSTRUMENTS

Before the piano was invented, harpsichords were the most popular keyboard instruments. The strings inside a harpsichord are plucked, making it sound completely different to a piano. Then, in 1700, an Italian called Bartolomeo Cristofori came up with a way for the strings to be hit with a hammer rather than plucked, creating a smooth and pleasing sound. This was the invention of the piano.

Harpsichords were favourite instruments in courts and parlour rooms until the 1800s.

UNDER THE LID

Underneath the lid of any piano are two sets of strings – a set of shorter strings for the high, treble notes, and a set of long strings for the bass notes. Test this for yourself – find an elastic band and stretch it tight. You can create a musical sound by plucking the band. If you stretch it tighter or make it shorter, it makes a higher sound. Depending on the length and tightness of the elastic band, you can create different notes.

String   Hammer

Inside a piano, each note is made with a set of two or three strings, each with its own hammer.

With the lid raised, it's easy to spot the long (bass) and short (treble) strings inside a grand piano.

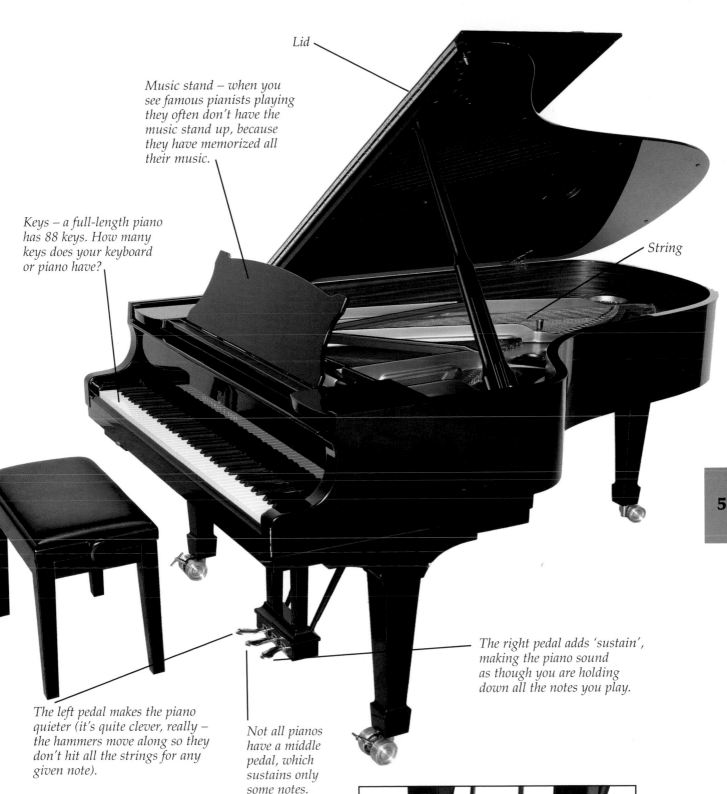

Lid

Music stand – when you see famous pianists playing they often don't have the music stand up, because they have memorized all their music.

Keys – a full-length piano has 88 keys. How many keys does your keyboard or piano have?

String

The right pedal adds 'sustain', making the piano sound as though you are holding down all the notes you play.

The left pedal makes the piano quieter (it's quite clever, really – the hammers move along so they don't hit all the strings for any given note).

Not all pianos have a middle pedal, which sustains only some notes.

PEDALS

Depending on the piano that you play, you might have three pedals or two pedals. Each pedal has a different function, but as a beginner you will only use the right pedal.

GETTING STARTED

Practice and mental attitude enable us to improve with any hobby or skill. The most important thing to remember is that practice should be fun! It is all about enjoying music. Sometimes it is challenging, but you should always feel rewarded by your progress. Here are some top tips to get you going…

Planning Counts!

Before you start practising, plan out what you are going to do:

- *Which exercises or scales are you going to warm up with?*
- *What sections of your pieces are you going to work on and practise?*
- *What piece are you going to reward yourself with playing at the end of your practice? (This should be something you can already play and you really enjoy!)*

The Five Times Rule

This rule really works! If you can play a tricky bit of a piece five times in a row, then you have got it nailed! If you make a mistake though, you go back to zero!

Regular as Clockwork

Try to do 10–15 minutes' practice every day.

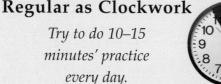

Slow Down!

Do everything slowly until you get the hang of it. If it all gets too much, then have a break and try again later.

Mental Attitude

It's really important to want to improve. Practising requires a certain amount of discipline, but the rewards are definitely worth it and you will develop a skill you will have for the rest of your life.

PREPARING TO PLAY

Since you will be sitting down to play, it's very important to make sure that you sit properly at the piano. Getting your posture right will also help you to get comfortable and relax, and running through a few warm-up exercises before you start will get you up and running.

SITTING UP STRAIGHT

A correct posture helps you to remain alert and help improve your playing. Make sure that the stool you sit on does not move or swivel and is not too high or too low. You should be able to reach the keys comfortably without having to lean forward.

WARMING UP

If you were going to run a race you would warm up first to ensure you were at your best. Make sure to warm up your fingers before you play the piano and you'll get a lot more out of your time!

Warm-up Routine

- *Pick different warm-up exercises for each practice.*
- *Pick a couple of scales to run through.*
- *Once you can play the warm-ups, challenge yourself to play them faster.*
- *Try them out legato and staccato (see pages 16–19).*

Technical Terms

Signs and symbols on a music score tell you the 'dynamics' of a piece of music – how loud or quiet to play.

≡ – 'piano' – *quiet*

≡ – 'mezzo-piano' – *quite quiet*

≡ – 'mezzo-forte' – *quite loud*

— – 'forte' – *loud*

– 'fortissimo' – *very loud*

'crescendo' – *get louder*

CODA
'diminuendo' – *get quieter*

RHYTHM

If you take your pulse, you can feel your heart beating regularly. This steady pulse is like a beat in music. Different types of notes are held for different numbers of beats to create different rhythms.

GET INTO THE GROOVE

1

Tap along to a favourite piece of music – once you're in time, you've got the beat of the music.

Note Lengths

o   *Semibreve (or whole note) = 4 beats*

♩   *Minim (or half note) = 2 beats*

♪   *Crotchet (or quarter note) = 1 beat*

♪   *Quaver (or eighth note) = ½ beat*

♪   *Semiquaver (or sixteenth note = ¼ beat*

♫   *Two quavers = ½ + ½ = 1 beat*

Quavers

Don't be tempted to play quavers as fast as you can. Usually, quavers are grouped in twos or fours, so practise clapping two claps to every beat – that's a quaver.

3

Have a go at clapping this rhythm:

4

If all music was written as one long line of notes, like the one above, it would get really confusing. Lines divide up music into 'bars' of equal numbers of beats. Clap this rhythm:

5

Bar lines should be invisible to the listener – don't pause when you get to them. Now clap out this rhythm. Can you recognize what children's nursery rhyme it comes from?

TIME SIGNATURES

Not all pieces have four beats in a bar. At the beginning of every piece of music the 'time signature' tells you how many and what type of beats are in each bar.

The top number tells us how many beats are in the bar.

The bottom number tells us what type of beat it is. A '4' means it's a quarter note (a crotchet), and an '8' means it's an eighth note (a quaver).

See if you can clap the following exercises:

Dotty Notes!

When you see a dot after a note it means 'hold this note for half its value again'. So a minim with a dot would be 2 beats + 1 beat (half a minim) = 3 beats.

♩.   3 beats

♪.   1½ beats (or 3 quavers)

Rests

These are the symbols for rests in music:

Rest for whole bar or 4 beats   ▬

Rest for 2 beats   ▬

Rest for 1 beat   𝄽

Rest for a quaver (½ beat)   𝄾

9

TREBLE NOTATION

In music, notes are written on five lines called a 'stave'. Treble notation shows the high notes above middle C on the piano keyboard, which are usually played with your right hand. Dive in and learn how to find these notes on the keyboard!

NOTES ON THE TREBLE STAVE

Ledger lines – extra lines used when the notes go beyond the five lines of the stave.

Stave

C D E F G A B C D E F G A B C

This is the treble clef sign and usually shows notes above middle C that your right hand plays.

NOTES ON THE PIANO KEYBOARD

C D E F G A B D E F G A B C

Middle C

BASIC HAND POSITION

1

Each digit on your right hand has a number. Your thumbs are one and the numbers work outwards. Make a mental note and then place your hand on the piano keyboard.

Middle C

2

The basic hand position is your right hand thumb on middle C and each finger on the notes above it. Middle C is the note C in the middle of the piano.

3

Always make sure your hand is in a good rounded position. An excellent way to check this is to put your hand on your knee and then lift it onto the keys – keep that rounded shape and keep your wrist flat.

4

Test your knowledge of notes on the piano keyboard by finding and playing these treble clef notes below as quickly as possible.

C   D   E   F   G   A   B   C   D   E   F   G   A   B   C

5

Play through these treble clef exercises. It might be a good idea to clap through the rhythms first.

Ready Reference

Refer back to these pages as you work through the book – they will help you work out any notes you are unsure of.

EXERCISE 11.1

EXERCISE 11.2

EXERCISE 11.3

EXERCISE 11.4

TREBLE NOTATION

BASS NOTATION

Now for the bass clef. Bass notation shows the low notes below middle C on the piano keyboard, which are usually played with your left hand.

NOTES ON THE BASS STAVE

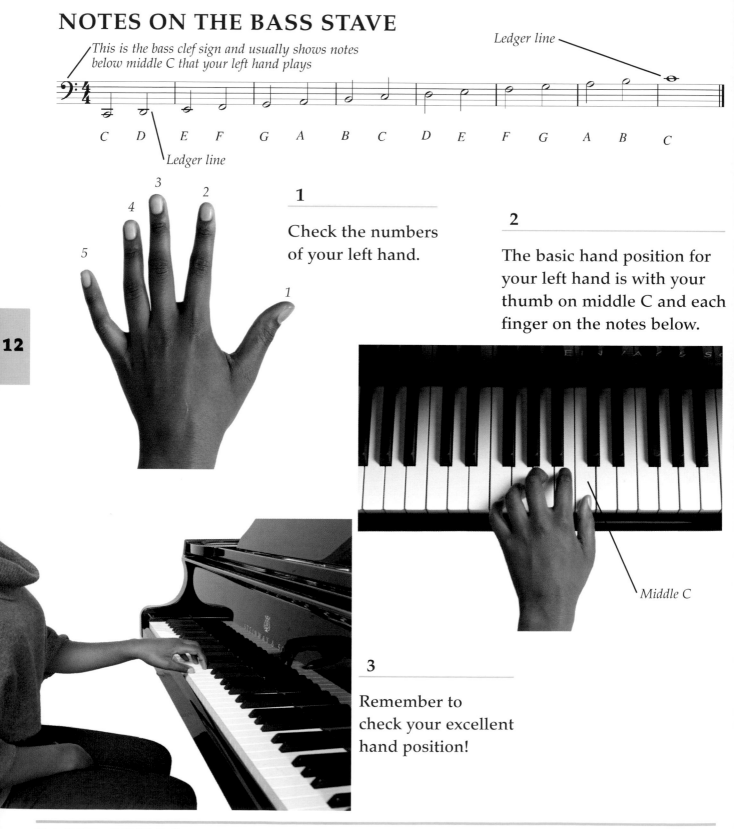

This is the bass clef sign and usually shows notes below middle C that your left hand plays

Ledger line

C D E F G A B C D E F G A B C

Ledger line

1

Check the numbers of your left hand.

2

The basic hand position for your left hand is with your thumb on middle C and each finger on the notes below.

Middle C

3

Remember to check your excellent hand position!

12

4

Have a go at finding and playing these
bass clef notes as quickly as you can!

5

Now have a go at these bass clef exercises. Clap through
the rhythms first to get an idea of how they go.

EXERCISE 13.1

EXERCISE 13.2

13

EXERCISE 13.3

EXERCISE 13.4

HANDS TOGETHER

Putting both hands together is the first really big step you will take when learning to play the piano. Almost any piece of music you can name has separate parts for right and left hands, so mastering this technique will unlock a whole new world of music and enjoyment. Remember, practice makes perfect!

BEGINNING SLOWLY

Here are two exercises with basic hand positions (thumbs on middle C) to practise hands together:

1

Look at the time signature. How many beats are in a bar?

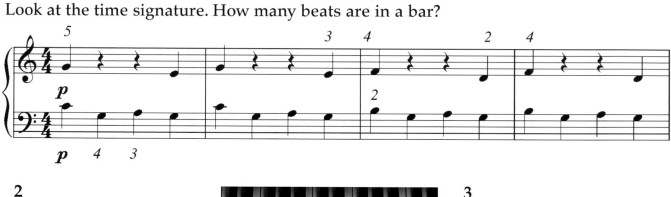

2

Slowly practise each hand separately, using The Five Times Rule (*see* page 6).

Middle C

3

Put the two separate hands together. Start very slowly at first, putting the parts together, bar by bar.

ONE MORE EXERCISE

Here is another exercise to practise your hands-together technique:

SHIFTING HAND POSITIONS

As you get better at playing, you will find more pieces that ask you to move your hand into a different position, onto a new set of notes, within the same piece! Don't fear – so long as you work out where your hands start, and where and when they change position, you will be fine.

Master the Technique

Usually, if you have to move more than one note, your hand 'jumps' position. However, when moving up or down a scale, you can just slip your thumb underneath your hand onto the next note (RH going up/LH going down), or move your finger over your thumb (RH going down/LH going up).

When 'jumping', lift your hand completely off the keyboard – try to make the movement as positive as it can be.

Be sure to give yourself enough room when passing your thumb under your hand.

'THUMB UNDER'

These exercises will help you to practise changing hand position:

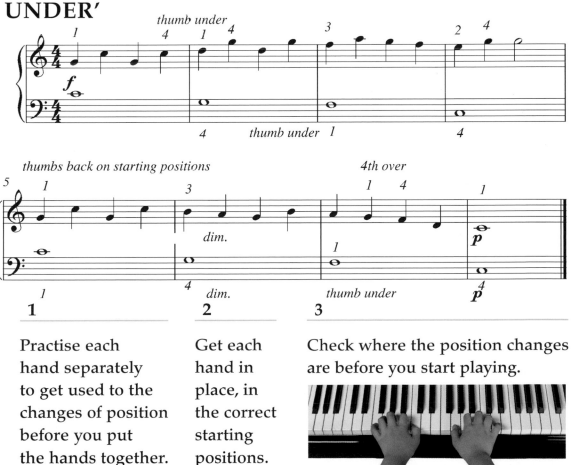

1

Practise each hand separately to get used to the changes of position before you put the hands together.

2

Get each hand in place, in the correct starting positions.

3

Check where the position changes are before you start playing.

PLAYING LEGATO

Now you have got to grips with basic rhythm, treble and bass notes, as well as hands together, you are ready to add some style to your playing. Legato is a smooth and polished playing style, that will have you sounding like a professional.

SMOOTH AND STYLISH LEGATO

There are lots of different ways to play a piece of music – loudly or softly, animated or laid back, slurred or choppy. 'Legato' means to play smoothly, with all the notes running together sweetly, making sure there are no overlapping of notes or gaps between them.

Smoothly Does It

To get the best results, try to keep a good hand position and let your fingers move smoothly without getting tense.

Have a go at playing these exercises as smoothly as possible – imagine each finger rocking from one note to the next.

D.C. al CODA
CODA ⊕

D.C. al Coda *means first go back to the beginning until you get to the* CODA *sign (which is the circle with the cross) and then go to the* CODA *bars to finish the piece.*

STARLIGHT:

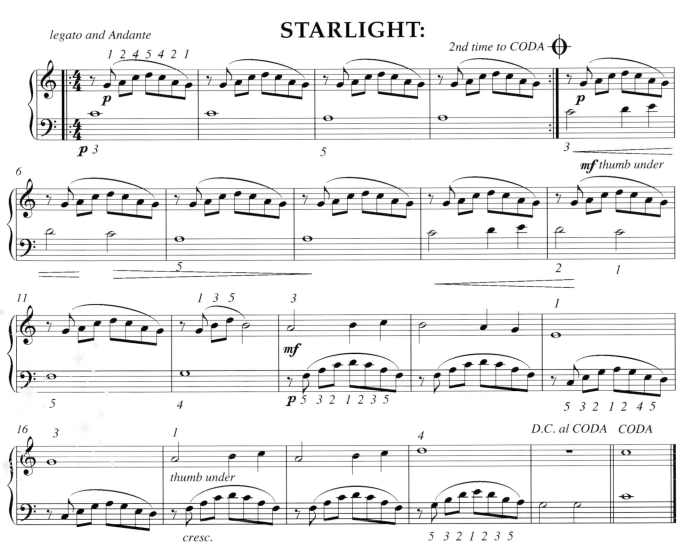

1

Work out what position your hands start in before you start to play.

2

Practise each hand separately first, making sure the notes are correct.

3

Check your hand movements in the piece – here are the hands at bar 15.

4

Now bring both hands together and practise very slowly.

PLAYING STACCATO

Staccato notes are short and separated – you should be able to hear a gap in between them. When you see a note with a dot above or below it, it means play it in a staccato style.

CHOPPY STACCATO

1

To play in a staccato style you need to imagine that you are bouncing a ball, keeping your wrist relaxed. Have a go at this, with your hand in a playing position.

2

Now have a go at playing this way – try it with every finger of both hands. Is one hand better than the other?

3

Now have a go at playing these exercises in a staccato style.

Mind Tricks

Think about the piano being really, really hot… the minute you touch it – ouch! Take your fingers straight off!

HAPPY HOPPING

Hand Position

Remember to keep a good hand position with your wrist relaxed. Try not to move your arms up and down when your fingers play the staccato notes.

1

Practise each hand separately.

2

The trick with this piece is to capture the rhythm. At the beginning, think 'left, right, left, right,' etc. In bar three, think 'left, right, left, right, left, right, together, right'. Simple!

3

In bar seven, you need to play two notes with your right hand at the same time. Practise this separately … and remember to keep your wrist relaxed.

TAKING IT FURTHER

Piano pieces come with all sorts of different time signatures. You have already tackled time signatures with three and four beats to a bar, but the more different time signatures you play, the more skilful you will become!

DAYDREAMING

1

Place your hands on the keyboards in the starting position for *Daydreaming*.

2

At bar 13, your hands should be in this position.

SHAPES IN MOTION

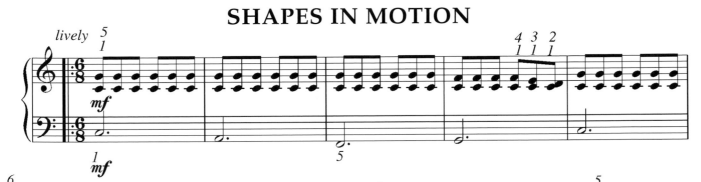

Time Check

Remember that 6/8 means there are six quavers or eighth notes in a bar.

1

Prepare yourself to start this piece by placing your hands on the keyboard in this pattern.

2

Think about getting the notes right, then add dynamics. In bar nine, you reach this position.

TAKING IT FURTHER

FINGER STRENGTH

Keen football or netball players have to keep in shape, and there is no difference for piano players! Keeping your fingers in tip-top condition is essential, so here are exercises you can do to help your fingers gain strength, agility and suppleness, while staying tension-free!

SHAPE UP!

A good exercise is to choose a finger and step from that finger to another finger a few times before moving on to the next. Try the following exercise using your little finger on your right hand:

EXERCISE 22.1

Now try starting with your 4th finger going up to your 5th, and then to your 3rd, 2nd and 1st.

Building Agility

Concentrate on playing the notes evenly. Check that your hand position is rounded and it's your fingers doing the work.

EXERCISE 22.2

MUSICAL SIGNS

There are so many things to think about when you are playing a piece of music – the notes, the rhythm, the time signature, dynamics and, on top of all that, musical signs and expressions that tell you how to play the piece! Here are some meanings of signs you might come across:

Accents – When you see this sign above or below a note, it means 'emphasize the note and make it stand out'.

Repeat – We have already come across this sign in the pieces we have played. When you see this, it means 'repeat' or 'go back to'.

start repeat

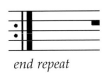

end repeat

D.C. *al Fine* – Go back to the beginning of the piece until you reach the word '*Fine*', which means 'finish' or 'stop'!

D.C. al Fine

TEMPO INSTRUCTIONS

Instructions on how fast to play a piece are usually put at the beginning, unless it marks a change of pace in the tune. For historical reasons, most instructions are in Italian. Here are some of their meanings:

Technical Terms

Presto – Very fast tempo

Vivace – Lively and fast tempo

Allegro – Fast tempo

Allegretto – Fairly fast tempo

Moderato – Moderate tempo

Andante – Quite slow, at a walking pace

Adagio – Slow tempo

Largo – Even slower!

rit. – This is short for ritardando *and means 'gradually slow down'. You usually see it at the end of a piece of music.*

accel. – This is short for accelerando *and means 'speed up'!*

THE BLACK KEYS

The black keys open up a whole range of new sounds and moods on the piano. These keys are called 'sharps' and 'flats', and they raise or lower a note by half a tone. The signs that tell you to play them are called 'accidentals', even though there is nothing accidental about it if the music tells you to play them.

ACCIDENTALS ON THE PIANO KEYBOARD

There are three signs that are used when playing black keys – they are called 'accidentals'.

1

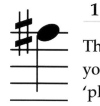

This sign is called a 'sharp'. When you see it before a note, it means 'play the next key to the right'.

2

Practise finding sharp notes by playing these notes on the piano:

3

This sign is called a 'flat'. When you see it before a note, it means 'play the next key to the left'.

4

Have a go at playing these flat notes on the piano:

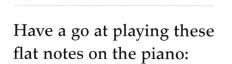

5

This sign is the 'natural'. When you see it, play the note without a sharp or a flat. If a note has been sharp, the natural sign 'resets' it to normal.

Don't Get Caught Out!

When you see a sharp or a flat in front of a note, you play every matching note in that bar in the same way, but remember that when you get to the next bar it goes back to normal. Test your skills and try not to get caught out when playing the exercise below.

MORE ADVANCED SKILLS

ELEPHANT PARADE

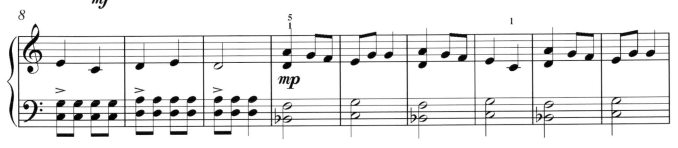

1

Put your knowledge into practice and have a stab at playing this piece of music. Your fingers start in this position (right).

Musical Direction

Remember to look out for the accents and the speed change at the end. This gives the piece a bit of excitement. (Turn back to page 23 for a reminder of what these signs mean.)

ORIENTAL MIST

Trade Secrets

This piece only uses black keys. Remember that all accidentals last for the whole bar unless cancelled by a natural sign. Try holding down the right sustain pedal for the entire piece – it really adds to the effect.

1

Oriental Mist starts with your hands in this position. Remember to play legato.

2

Practise playing both hand parts separately before bringing them together. At bar 11 your hands should look like this (right).

M O R E   A D V A N C E D   S K I L L S

26

ALLEYCATS

with a swing feel

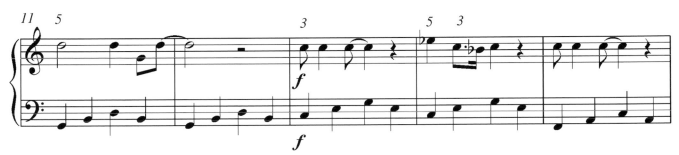

Purr-fect Rhythm

Practise the right hand rhythm carefully. Your left hand plays the same pattern of notes but moves to different positions on the keyboard.

1

Test your sight reading by playing through the piece slowly. Start with your fingers in this position.

2

Concentrate on getting the swing feel in both parts. This is how your hands look in bar 13.

THE BLACK KEYS (CONTINUED)

SCALES

Scales are the core exercises of any skilled pianist. They allow you to gain fluidity and control in your playing. Learning scales can seem like hard work, but they are really important in helping you to command the keyboard!

C MAJOR SCALE

1

The simplest scale to learn is C major. Remember to practise each hand separately first and then try to put them together slowly.

There are several reasons why it is important to learn and practise scales:

• They are excellent warm-ups.
• They help you recognize and play in different keys.
• They allow you to become familiar with the keyboard.
• They help train your brain to remember patterns.
• Lots of pieces use scale patterns, so you will already know them when you come to play them.

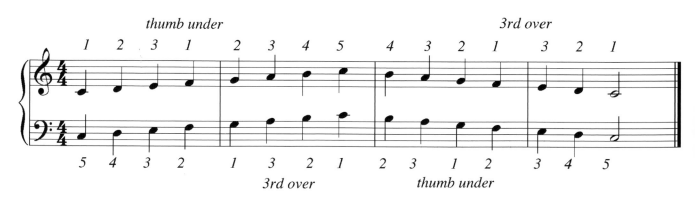

Tips for Practising Scales:

• *Make sure to play your scales at the same speed.*
• *The notes need to be really even – listen carefully when you are playing them.*
• *Make sure that your wrist stays relaxed and in the same position as it moves up and down the piano.*
• *Certain notes or patterns can help you – for instance in C major,*
finger 3 on both hands lands together, first on E and then on A.

KEY SIGNATURES

Pieces of music can be in different 'keys' – and each key has a different number of sharps or flats to make its characteristic sound. A key signature, which is written at the beginning of a piece, tells you which notes are sharp and flat.

THE KEY OF G MAJOR

Key signature for G major.
All the Fs are sharp.

THE KEY OF F MAJOR

Key signature for F major.
All the Bs are flat.

Handy Signatures

A key signature at the start of a piece of music means that every time you play a particular note it is sharp or flat, saving you the trouble of reading a sharp or flat every time you play the note.

Tonics

The main note in the key is the first note in the scale, which is called the 'tonic'.

G MAJOR SCALE
1

Place your fingers in the starting position shown. Remember all the F notes are sharp.

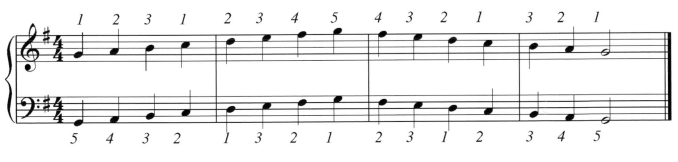

F MAJOR SCALE
1

F major starting position.
Remember all the B notes are flat.

MINOR SCALES

W̲hen you listen to pieces or scales in a major key they sound happy, but when you listen to them in a minor key they sound sad. Here are some scale patterns for minor keys.

A MINOR SCALE

1

The A minor scale looks like this. Place your fingers in their starting positions and practise playing the scale evenly.

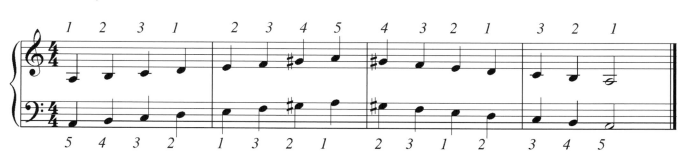

D MINOR SCALE

1

This is the scale of D minor. The starting positions for your fingers are shown on the right.

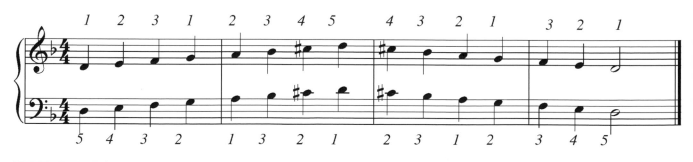

Relative Minor and Relative Major Keys

C major and A minor have the same key signature (no sharps or flats). For each major scale, there is a minor scale which has the same key signature – because of this, we describe them as 'related'. So you would say that A minor is the 'relative minor' of C major and C major is the 'relative major' of A minor.

SCALE EXERCISES

Try these scale exercises to add variety to your scale practice.

EXERCISE 31.1

EXERCISE 31.2

CHORDS & ARPEGGIOS

When you play several notes together on the piano, you are playing a 'chord'. These solid combinations can be broken up to create beautiful cascades of notes called 'arpeggios'. Chords appear more often in pieces as you get better at playing the piano, so they are definitely worth getting to grips with.

HOW TO PLAY CHORDS

To play the main chord for any key signature, play the main note of the scale (the tonic), together with the third note and the fifth note.

1

Put your right-hand thumb on middle C with a relaxed hand position. Then play your thumb, third and fifth finger at the same time – you have just played the chord of C major.

2

Have a go at the following chords. Remember to check the key signatures first.

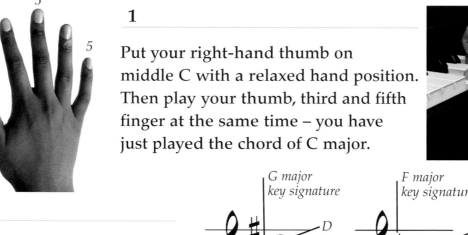

G major key signature
D
B
G
G major triad

F major key signature
C
A
F
F major triad

A minor key signature
E
C
A
A minor triad

HOW TO PLAY ARPEGGIOS

Arpeggios are when you play the notes that make up a chord separately, so that you can hear each note in turn in a particular pattern.

1

Place your hands on the keyboard with the fingering shown below. Then play one note after another, remembering to check the fingering. Practise hands separately first, before putting them together.

MORE ADVANCED SKILLS

2

This is a minor arpeggio, which means it uses these notes of the minor scale.

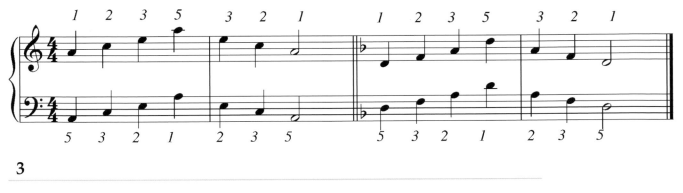

3

Once you feel ready, try this exercise, which uses eighth-note quavers.

HOW TO PLAY BROKEN CHORDS

Broken chords also play the notes that make up a chord, but in a different pattern to an arpeggio.

1

Have a go at the following broken chord in C major. Once you have learnt the fingering, play a D minor broken chord (thumb and 5th finger on D), an A minor broken chord (thumb and 5th on A) and an F major broken chord (thumb and 5th on F).

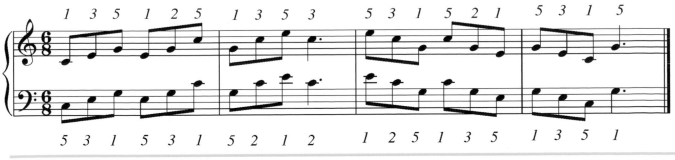

SIGHTREADING

Imagine someone putting a piece of music in front of you and being able to play it without having to slowly work out the notes, the hand positions, the key signatures, the time signatures… All of this is possible, with a little work and practice.

HOW TO SIGHTREAD

You may not have realized it, but you have already built up your sightreading skills by reading and practising the exercises in this book. Here are a few tips on what to look for when you see a piece for the first time.

1

Check the time signature.

2

Check the key signature. Then scan quickly through the piece to see if any notes are sharp or flat.

3

Spot any position changes before you start and work out how you are going to play them.

4

Check the direction on tempo and start your playing at a comfortable speed.

> ## Sightreader's Guide:
>
> • *Look for repeating patterns.*
> • *Try to spot chords and arpeggios that you already know.*
> • *Look for any change of dynamics.*

EXERCISE 34.1

MORE ADVANCED SKILLS

MORE SIGHTREADING EXERCISES

Practise your sightreading with the exercises below:

EXERCISE 35.1

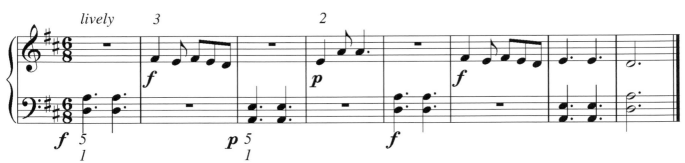

EXERCISE 35.2

EXERCISE 35.3

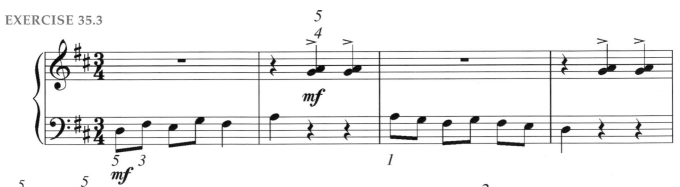

TRAIN YOUR EARS

Having a 'good pair of ears' is an important part of being a musician – they will help you to keep a steady pulse, recognize wrong notes, improve your singing voice and even enable you to play a piece of music just by listening to it.

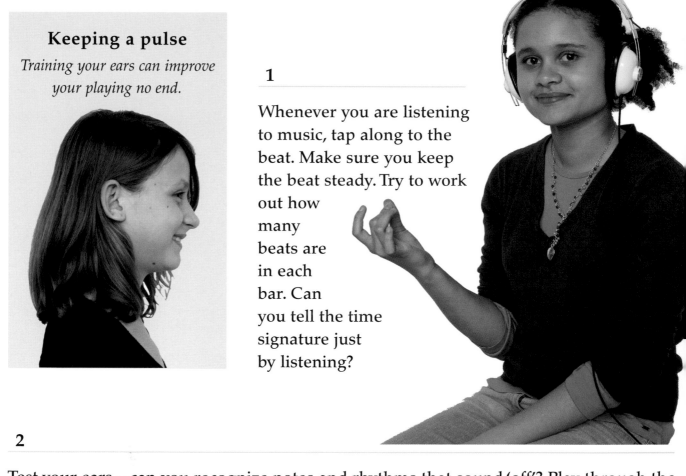

Keeping a pulse
Training your ears can improve your playing no end.

1

Whenever you are listening to music, tap along to the beat. Make sure you keep the beat steady. Try to work out how many beats are in each bar. Can you tell the time signature just by listening?

2

Test your ears – can you recognize notes and rhythms that sound 'off'? Play through the following phrases, which are taken from pieces in this book, and see if you can work out wrong notes or rhythms. You may need to play through the original once or twice first.

PHRASE FROM *SHAPES IN MOTION* (PAGE 21)

PHRASE FROM *ELEPHANT PARADE* (PAGE 25)

MORE ADVANCED SKILLS

DEVELOPING YOUR SINGING

Singing is a great way to improve your musical ear,
as it helps you to 'hear' the notes in your head.

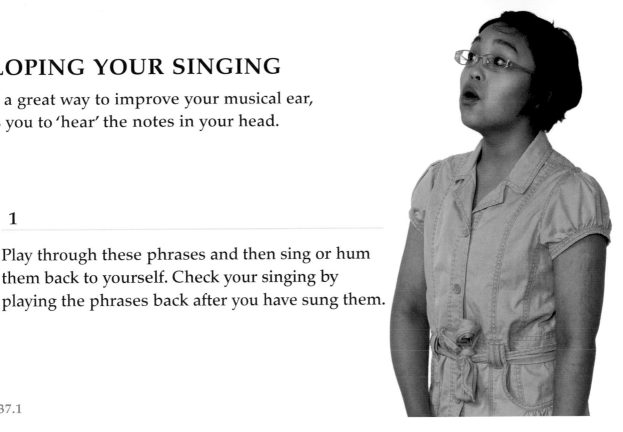

1

Play through these phrases and then sing or hum
them back to yourself. Check your singing by
playing the phrases back after you have sung them.

EXERCISE 37.1

EXERCISE 37.2

TRAINING BOOT CAMP

1

With practice, you will be able to figure out tunes that you have heard. Begin by
thinking of a song that you know and see if you can work out how to play it on the
piano. The more you practise, the quicker and more accurate you will become!

PIANO PIECES

The pieces on the following pages use the techniques you have learnt in this book. Remember to flip back to the basics pages if you are not sure about anything.

LAZY DAYS

1

Place your hands on the keys as shown. This piece has a laid-back feel. Concentrate on getting the left-hand slurs just right. Try to play legato style (*see* page 16).

2

At bar 13, your fingers look like this.

TANGO EXPRESS

1

Start with your fingers in this position. Practise both of your hands separately, paying particular attention to the right-hand part.

2

Try it hands together, slowly, bar by bar, using the Five Times Rule (*see* page 6). By bar 13, your hands will be in this position.

3

Now add in all the colourful bits – the dynamics and the staccato stabs to get that sassy tango feeling.

Stab that Rhythm!

The staccato notes in the left hand make a rhythm typical of tango.

SLIMY UNDERGROUND

This piece uses the otherworldly sound of the 'chromatic scale' – a scale made up of all the white keys and black notes next to each other. Now place your fingers in the starting position (left) and play.

with imagination!

Acciaccaturas

The last two bars contain two 'grace notes' called 'acciaccaturas' (say 'ak-chak-a-to-rah').
Play these notes immediately before the main note without any gap between.

SUNNY DAYS

1

This is a happy-sounding piece, so play it brightly. Start with your hands as shown (right) and practise both parts separately and slowly.

Key Signature

Don't forget the F sharps in this piece.

2

In bar 11, your hands will be tinkling over the keys in this position. Look out for the CODA at the end.

SLIMY UNDERGROUND & SUNNY DAYS

THE SNAKE CHARMER

Accidentals Will Happen

Remember that 'accidentals' are sharp or flat notes, most often played on the black keys.

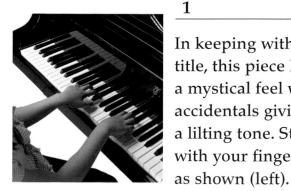

1

In keeping with the title, this piece has a mystical feel with accidentals giving it a lilting tone. Start with your fingers as shown (left).

2

Practise both hands separately, paying particular attention to the right-hand part. The finger position in bar nine is shown (right).

Starting position

Bb BOOGIE

1

'Boogie woogie' and 'stride' piano are modern musical forms that really rock! Start slowly with your fingers in this position (speed can come later).

CLOCKWORK

1

Start with your fingers in the position shown (right). Begin slowly, concentrating on getting the rhythm of the piece correct. The more you practise, the more fluent your playing will become.

Right-hand Shape

Keep your right hand in the same shape through most of this piece, by simply moving it from note to note.

2

Once you get both hands working together, everything will 'click'. Your fingers should hit this position in bar 11 (right).

PAVEMENT CRACKS

Here's a piece for you to try all by yourself. It will test your sightreading and all the skills you have learned in this book.

Watch the Hands!

This piece uses many hand positions – scan through the music and identify where they arise. Then make sure you practise them first.

GREAT PIANO PLAYERS

All pianists play for their own enjoyment, as well as (hopefully) the enjoyment of their family and friends! For some talented people, playing becomes a career. Rachmaninoff and Oscar Peterson were both famous and successful pianists and composers, who played to huge audiences all over the world.

SERGEI RACHMANINOFF

Rachmaninoff was born in Russia, in 1873 and died in Beverley Hills, California, in 1943.

As well as being a fantastic pianist, Rachmaninoff was a famous composer. Some of his most famous compositions are his Piano Concertos Nos. 2 and 3 and a piece called *Rhapsody on a Theme by Paganini* (1934). Rachmaninoff was a tall man, over 1.8 metres and had huge hands. It is thought that Rachmaninoff could play a chord of C, Eb, G, C and G with one hand! That's pretty amazing and very useful if you are a pianist.

OSCAR PETERSON

Oscar Peterson was born in Canada in 1925 and died in the USA in 2007.

Oscar Emmanuel Peterson (or OP to his friends) was one of the finest jazz pianists and composers to have lived. He recorded his first single when he was 19 and went on to record 200 albums and win eight Grammy awards. That's pretty good going! He was known for his energetic and virtuosic performances. See if you can find a recording of him and have a listen.

How to Progress With Your Playing

- *Get into a regular routine of practising, using the tips in this book.*
- *Don't give up if you sometimes find it hard – keep trying!*
- *Find a good teacher, who can explain any hard techniques to you and guide your learning.*
- *Always play some music that you really like (this will motivate you to practise).*
- *Finally, always ENJOY IT!*

GLOSSARY

accel – get faster, gradually

accent – stress the note

accidental – an accidental changes the pitch of a note

adagio – slow tempo

allegro – fast tempo

allegretto – fairly fast tempo

andante – quite slow tempo

dynamics – how loud or quiet the music should be played

flat – play the next key (usually black) to the left

key signatures – how many sharps and/or flats in a piece

largo – very slow tempo

legato – smoothly

moderato – moderate tempo

natura – play the original note

presto – very fast tempo

repeat – repeat the section between the repeat signs

rit – slow down, gradually

sharp – play the next key (usually black) to the right

staccato – detached notes, played punchily

tempo – the pace of the music – how fast or slow it goes

time signature – how many beats, and of what type, in a bar

tonic – the main, and first, note of a scale or key signature

triad – a three-note chord

vivace – lively and fast tempo

LISTINGS

Contact your local music service to enquire about individual piano lessons.
Federation of Musical Services (www.thefms.org)
European Association of Piano Teachers (www.epta-uk.org)
www.uk-piano.org also lists qualified piano teachers in the UK

www.piano.com has links throughout the world to various aspects of piano playing, including how to find a teacher, finding sheet music and learning about other pianists.

www.musictechteacher.com features games and fun quizzes

The website addresses are correct at the time of publishing. However, due to the ever-changing nature of the Internet, websites and content may change. Some websites can contain links that are unsuitable for children. The publisher is not responsible for changes in content or website addresses. We advise that Internet searches are supervised by an adult.